COUNTRY OF AIR

COUNTRY OF AIR

POEMS BY

RICHARD JONES

COPPER CANYON PRESS · PORT TOWNSEND

Acknowledgments

The Arts Journal: "The Hearing Aid"; *Chariton Review*: "The Fire"; *Cimarron Review*: "Moving Day"; *Crazyhorse*: "Times Like This"; *Crosscurrents*: "The Decoy"; *Empty Shelves*: "The Danger of Escaping"; *Iris*: "A Boy's Body"; *Kansas Quarterly*: "The Spiders"; *Manhattan Poetry Review*: "The Mechanic"; *New Letters*: "Looking at My Father," "The Horses," and "A Beginning"; *Northern Lights*: "The Gift," "The Solipsist's Self Portraits," "The Insects," and "Life After Death"; *Pembroke Magazine*: "Cloudburst," "Passion," and "Waiting"; *Poetry Now*: "The Letter" and "For My Friends"; *Quarry West*: "Riding the Train" and "The Waiting Room"; *Second Street Anthology*: "Wings" and "Mrs. Green"; *Virginia Quarterly Review*: "The Bell"; *Willow Springs*: "The Wounded One" and "The Idle Fleet."

"The Bell," "Bread Crumbs," "The Letter," and "The Spiders" originally appeared in *Windows and Walls* (Adastra Press, 1982). "The Mechanic," "For My Friends," and "Times Like This" originally appeared in *Innocent Things* (Adastra Press, 1985).

Publication of this book was made possible in part
by a grant from the National Endowment for the Arts.
Copper Canyon Press is in residence with Centrum
on Fort Worden State Park.

Copper Canyon Press
P.O. Box 271
Port Townsend
Washington 98368

CONTENTS

III. PARADISE ON FIRE

You must grieve for this right now…
if you are going to say "I lived."
— *Nazim Hikmet*

The Bell

In the tower the bell
is alone, like a man
in his room,
thinking and thinking.

The bell is made of iron.
It takes the weight
of a man
to make the bell move.

Far below, the bell feels
hands on a rope.
It considers this.
It turns its head.

Miles away,
a man in his room
hears the clear sound,
and lifts his head to listen.

I

Times Like This

Child in Woods

From inside my house I hear,
across the pasture, beyond the lake,
a boy hidden in pine woods
screaming, "goddamn, goddamn."
It's my neighbor's boy,
an angel-faced kid of eight,
yelling at the world.

I know those woods well.
Sunlight pours down through the branches
stained yellow and green and warm as love.
In those woods, a man
can walk out of the shadow of his life
and stand in shafts of sunlight,
the body numinous.

But the child is screaming.
What does he care that the day is perfect?
He's falling in a frenzy to the forest floor,
rolling around on soft pine needles,
pretending, screaming, killing some animal
only he can see.

I listen to the boy for a long time.
And though I know he'll soon rise up,
exhausted, his demons departed,
though I know he'll return home,
pine dust in his hair,

to the ones who worship him,
who make their home a temple
for the living paradise which is childhood,
though I know he is just a boy,
I can't help but hear

the man in the child's voice,
the man who invites his troubles,
his screaming like a prayer,
an invocation, calling the pain
which will come, and by which
his life will be defined.

The Wounded One

Geese crossing the corn fields,
gunshots coming from the woods,
the sky changing from blue to red
as the sun goes down. Geese cry out
and keep flying. I see them running
from gunfire, jostling one another,
sticking together, bound to one another
by fear and love and history. One bird
drops out of the V, calling out, like the others,
who turn as one for a moment, then rise again
to cross the ridge, leaving the wounded one behind.
She drops, flies low, struggling past my garden,
where I stand watching as she flies to the lake.
I hear her falling into the water,
hear men and dogs in the woods,
birds calling to one another beyond the ridge.
I cross the field to the lake,
following the cries of the bird,
and find her in the shallows of the marsh grass,
head held high, water stained red, her body
pushing itself around in circles.
I wade into the water, cold water, and hear
my breath coming faster. She hears it
and tries to lift up onto the opposite shore.
I'm coming to save her, or to bury her.
But she is alive,

and terrified.
She retreats into the woods,
farther and farther away.
She is determined to live,
to see this life through, until it's finished.

The Birds

When I try to say something about the birds
living around my house, or about the jay
tearing the cold insides from a mouse
I murdered and tossed in the yard,
I find myself writing instead
about Anne, the secretary I knew
in New York. She was afraid of people.
Even when the phone rang,
she'd sometimes start crying
and lock herself in the ladies' room.

I bet Anne could write a poem about the birds
for me. She'd know what to say
about the cream-colored bird I saw yesterday,
the way it made me think not about birds,
how they starve in winter,
but about the life of the soul.

I'd like to know what happened to crazy Anne.
The last time I saw her was in Times Square, after work.
Snow was falling and for once she wasn't crying.
She said, "My best friend's been murdered."
She was staring at neon reflecting
on the wet pavement, the snow
falling as in a dream, repeating
the dead girl's name over and over,
the same as hers,
Anne, Anne....

The Mechanic

It's dark in the garage. The mechanic
goes down into the concrete grave
with his trouble light, while the day
rushes past outside on the highway.

Standing in the pit beneath an old engine,
he works patiently, with a kind of gentleness.
Looking up, he could be in a field at night
staring into the sky for answers.

In the afternoons, when the owners come back
for their cars, he stands around with the other men,
drinking beer, pushing one another around, cursing.
He works the kinks out of his neck, squints into the sun.

The Letter

The clerk in the post office stops
one minute, lays down
a handful of letters on the table
before the wall of wooden letter slots.

He removes his glasses and wipes them
with a handkerchief pulled from his pocket.
When he breathes on the glass,
he can see the fingerprint of the world.

As he cleans his glasses he thinks
of his son, of the boy's last letter,
the casual way he wrote, "Tomorrow
I'm going back to the front."

Today the country is at peace.
The clerk resumes his work.
He reads each envelope, the names
of strangers, and each minute

his grief begins again,
holding letters in his hand,
feeling them moving through the world,
breathless and white.

Mrs. Green

I opened and let her in –
Mrs. Green, our elderly neighbor,
drunk again and knocking on the door.
She wanted to nap on our sofa.
Her dressing gown open, I saw
how mournfully her empty breasts hung down.
Taking my arm to steady herself,
she called me by her husband's name.
He loved her, but didn't let her drink.
He hid the keys to her car.
Some nights I heard them arguing.
Often she went to the hospital.
The doctors put her back together
whenever she broke herself.

It's funny. Mr. Green
died years before she did.
She kept going.
She sleeps in my memory on our sofa.
And still inside her is the deep
fear and knowledge
that another night is coming,
the cold and the shaking.
Some nights I looked down
from my window, saw her
crawling around in the dark,
digging in our backyard for bottles she hid.
Looking up at my face and howling,
it seemed to me, when she found nothing.

Bread Crumbs

They knock with their Bibles
on your grandmother's front door.
One man presses his fat red face
against the screen, yelling,

but he can't see you.
The two of you
are a secret behind the sofa.
It's a little game
your grandmother has taught you:
when a salesman comes
you play silence and hiding and no money.

Your grandmother knows the virtue of patience.
The man on the porch will go away.
So you wait like a child waiting, head bowed,
for a prayer to end, when all you want

is to eat supper with her,
and, afterwards, sweep the table clean
the way she showed you,
one hand brushing bread crumbs into the other –

both hands filled,
just enough in each fist to open
the door and face the hungry day.

The Spiders

It took my father and me years to learn
how to talk. Now we don't say anything.
We touch each other from a distance,
two men carrying a ladder
we set against his house.

Along the coast, people live
in houses built on stilts,
so when the storms rage up the shore
the ocean passes safely underneath.

Spiders live there, too,
working their webs each day.
In one evening
they can cover the house
while he's inside, sleeping,
sprawled across the bed
as though he'd fallen there by accident
to finish the day.

When I visit my father,
we cover our faces with rags.
We mix poison.
I can't turn away,
holding the ladder so my father doesn't fall,
and, as he climbs away from me,
as I forgive us both,

I see that we have found
ourselves at last —
me on the earth, my father in the sky —
and I don't turn away from the spiders
or the poison blessing this house.

The Idle Fleet
James River, Virginia

The river below hard as steel,
a boy stands on the deck
of a mothballed battleship
and feels the wind in his hair.
He isn't thinking about history
and war. He doesn't care
that what saved us
has become old and useless,
each ship its own gray tombstone
anchored in the James.
It is enough for him
to be alive, to challenge
the other boys rowing out
to climb into the sky.
He knows it is better,
now, while he is alive,
not to think but to fling
himself into the air
and go flying,
become an angel,
let the simple air hold him
like the hand of God
until he falls,
with the others,
exploding into the water,
the dirty river accepting him
in its current, carrying him
into the future,
into his life as a man.

Riding the Train

Floating toward home, through the window
I see towns built around churches,
the dead a field of fenced-in names,
the blank stare of the stones;
and now, between church and cemetery,
the faces of children in a garden
who've stopped to watch the train pass through,
out into fields and open places.
There I see a pick-up turn off the main road
and lose itself in a gold cloud.
At the end of the lane, a woman
lives alone in a farmhouse.
She feels the earth trembling, the train
going by like a moment of anger.
She leans toward the window to see,
one hand parting the curtain,
one hand gripping the wheel of her chair.

Times Like This

She closes the gate
of the public garden
behind her, an autumn garden,
walled-in, without flowers,
only bare fruit trees
and the intimation
of bad weather.
I'm by myself on the bench,
the leaves, like the children
we talked about having,
racing back and forth
in the windy sunshine
at my feet. It's a scene
we know by heart –
the careful voices,
the careful good-byes.
We've learned it is better
not to talk at times like this
but to leave quietly when
we must, the only sound
the click of a lock.
The afternoon caught
between apple trees
twisted in thought
and pomegranates blooming
along the north wall,
I see she's gone for good.
I count the minutes,

the bricks in the wall,
the money I'll need next week,
the children we won't have.
This small garden
is the perfect size
for my angry heart,
for all the dark words
that created this silence,
for the emptiness
which will survive
in the solitude of desire,
and for the rough grace
which illuminates the soul,
poised between love and nothing.

The Fire

While the man next door rests in bed,
it begins:
the moment in the wiring gnawed by a mouse.
Flame opens like a seed, so small
it's almost impossible to see
even in the dark, even if you
were standing in the room
listening for it.
But no matter how small, fire
loves wood. It fills the rooms
with smoke the sleepers inhale,
smoke taking them deeper.

Next door, the man turns in bed,
then sits up.
He goes to the window.
He goes outside. The neighbor's house
sings with fire, light
dances in his face. He can't believe
what he sees
although someday he'll understand
how often this happens,
the infinite number
of lives and deaths he's slept through.

II

Country of Air

A Suicide

A few minutes ago,
on the roof,
she believed she had become
light enough to go dancing
in the country of air.
She imagined a hand
reaching out to her.
It was, finally, all she wanted.

On the street, people
turn away from her body,
her back broken
across the top of the fence.
They see her
as a worn-out coat
left behind on the iron railing,
forgotten by some silly girl
gone dancing.
The way her legs dangle down
it is easy to imagine

she was dancing.
The peaceful look on her face
makes it possible to believe
she is exhausted,
and sleeping now,
were it not for the fact
her eyes are slightly open,
seeming to see us.

The Gift

I've given you nothing
today, or yesterday, so tonight
I go out to the graveyard
in the rain to pick

the spring's first wildflowers –
daffodils a century old
growing wild over the graves.
I bend down and think of you

alone in the bed
and confess what I love:
darkness and the desire
to lie down here forever.

What have I to give anyone?
Even these stupid flowers
seem like a dead man's fist,
holding on and never letting go.

The Solipsist's Self-Portraits

I. THE BED

Drunk under the blanket,
the sheet pulled over my head,
the bed becomes my cloud,
floating high above you,
who are calling me back.
You say I am lost,
but I know where I am:
on a cloud so far away
no one can touch me,
no one can hurt me
because I'm not human:
I'm a deaf angel,
someone who will never hear you
or speak to you again.

2. PORTRAIT OF A MAN WALKING

Look how gracefully he moves,
strolling down the street
like a cloud, slipping
between people, past cars.
Even when faces rush forward
to greet him, he smiles,
and moves on, effortlessly,
like a ghost walking
through a wall, his life
falling away behind him,

a wake, a jetsam of facts
in an ocean of faces
he believes, he believes,
he's touched.

3. THE LIE

I am telling you a lie,
a great lie that goes on and on,
a lie as huge as a life,
a lie as strong as planks
used to build the hull of a ship,
a lie as sharp as the axe
that cuts the ropes
tied to the dock,
a lie as tall and empty
as the black sails
carrying me out to sea.
The lie is the captain
standing on the deck,
I, his prisoner,
locked in the hold.
The bars on the porthole frame
people gathered on the shore.
They are so far away I know
I will never see them again.
If they could hear me
I swear I'd tell the truth
this time, truth blooming

like a white rose
so beautiful no one would believe it.
But everyone is growing smaller,
a little bouquet in the distance.
They can't hear me,
or my plea to be forgiven,
or the last thing I said:
Take me back.

Cloudburst

Black shadows descend
on the garden
of tulips and daffodil

and mother runs down
the farmhouse steps,
her hand on her dress,

to save the white sheet
waving on the line.
It wants to blow away,

to fall into the dirt
where rain and earth
will wear it

to nothing,
a rag.
But mother hugs

the bedclothes tight,
like a baby she carries
into the house.

From far away
she calls
my name.

I see her
brush the raindrops
from her thick black hair.

Looking at My Father

When I come down
after searching for him in the attic
among the uniforms and the flight gear
to find him digging in his garden,
I don't see a pilot, I see a farmer,
a solid man built for standing on the earth.

He spent a lifetime flying,
but never talks about it,
the way a man won't tell his wife
of the mistress he once loved,
the secret story of his life,
what came between them.

My father's eyes are a faint blue,
the color of sky fading into nothing.
I imagine him looking down at us
from his country of air.
We are so small
from that great distance.

Wings

I loved the wings
on his flight jackets –
silver wings
I'd hold in my hand,
a silver star
where the heart should have been.
As a child,
I used to climb trees
to find him.
Trees are what I imagined
wings felt like
waving all around me.
I'd reach the top
and wait all day
for one white line
written in the sky,
for distant silver wings
to echo the sun,
the silence so bright
it hurt to look.

The Danger of Escaping

Sometimes I go too high,
sometimes I float out
beyond the white rope
that my body,
far below on the earth,
is patiently holding.
I barely can see
myself down there,
the husk of my flesh,
the heavy damp feel
of my skin, the way
I lie on my back
like a dead man
saying my name.
This is when I know
it is useless: I've gone
so high and so far
I'm afraid
I'll never come back.

Waiting

I've been waiting here so long
I've forgotten what it is I'm waiting for.
I've forgotten why I wait by the window
watching the road and listening.

Maybe someone's come already?
Maybe I hid in my room
when I heard the footsteps?
Maybe I'm not waiting, but hiding?

Or maybe it's impossible to hide
and someone is here with me now.
Maybe I'm already holding everyone in my arms
I'll ever love, or know, or be.

The Insects

When I write
the insects come
to bother me.
They dance in the light.
They make love,
their little wings
singing to each other.
But I have work to do.
I brush them away.
I don't mean to kill anyone,
but sometimes their bodies
leave brown smudges
on the paper under my hands.
You can't see this,
reading what I've written,
now, in this book.

For My Friends

Days are spent in the meadow brooding
over lives that go on without me

in the city. Friends meet
after work in bars and talk
about music and Marx and what is wrong
with American men. It is still light
when they go out among the crowds
on Columbus Avenue, walking uptown
to the Mexican restaurant, where the service is slow,
and you can sit all night in the courtyard
while empty plates pile up around you,
and night covers the square of sky
above you, and lights come on
everywhere, and the city is

alive, like this meadow in summer –
a million small things buzzing with life –
as I make my way back to the farmhouse in the dark.

Life After Death

What I envy in the open eyes
of the dead deer hanging down
from the rafters, its eyes
still wet and glassy, but locked now
into a vision of another life,
is the way it seems to be
staring at the moment when
it died. The blue light
falling through the window
into this smoke-filled room
is the same color as the mist
coming down off the mountain
that morning: the deer sees
men with guns,
but also sees, beyond them,
the endless mountains.

III

Paradise on Fire

A Boy's Body

He has a perfect body, this boy
in a checkered bathing suit
walking away from me
toward the lake,
his waist hard and slim as a girl's,
the muscular back and broad shoulders
already strong enough to bear sorrow and grief.
God knows what he's thinking about
as he strolls toward the water.
He sees, across the pasture,
two horses coming toward him.
His small heart –
people pound on the walls
to get in, to get out.
It makes him walk
a little awkwardly.
Like Michelangelo's David,
he has big feet
and large delicate hands.
When the hill slopes down
he picks up speed, begins to run,
his body gaining power,
almost beyond his control,
enough to kill,
or touch us with his love.

The Horses

The rain has come
and I cannot see the three horses
wandering in the pasture.
It's logical
to say they are still there,
huddled under the trees,
the rain turning to mist
as it falls through the branches.
I know nothing about horses
except that they will come back,
waiting for me by the fence,
bowing their sad and beautiful faces,
wanting to kiss my hand.
They stand all winter in silence.
It's like a dream I don't understand.
I walk outside and see,
as the rain turns to snow,
these slow lumbering horses
moving toward me,
the heavy walk
toward apples and sugar,
their heads hung low
with that miserable look
I somehow love·
but have never loved enough.

The Miscarriage

The day we lost the baby
and I came home
to find you
drugged, in pain,
the white nightgown
delicately shrouding your body,
I sat in the chair
at the foot of the iron bed
and listened to you cry.
I did not say much
except that it would be all right,
then cradled my arms carefully around you.
What did I know?
As I held you,
I felt I had been caught.
The brief light of our souls –
child too sad to show its face –
shone upon my life, revealing
all the things I'd done
that can and will be used
as evidence against me.

The Waiting Room

No one looks at anyone else.
No one speaks: we are sick.
We slouch, careful not to touch
one another, turning the pages
of magazines, pretending to read.
A man comes in but there are no chairs,
so he stands against the wall.
He looks out the window
wondering what disease
is buried in his body
like a treasure.
If life is a miracle,
then death is, too.
I look out the window.
The woman next to me
looks out the window.
Late winter afternoon.
Darkness coming down.
A nurse turns on another lamp,
keeping the room bright.
But the examining room is dark
as the doctor's eyes, hidden
behind the strongly focused beam
shooting out from the silver circle,
his face drawing nearer
to the sick one, light coming
out the center of his head.

Love for the Bottle

The house seems empty without you.
I let the dirty clothes pile up
soberly in the kitchen
and sit like a Puritan
in a straight-backed chair.
I don't know what to do
with my body, the way it wants
to carry me into the future
like a souvenir. I can't go
anywhere, I can't sleep,
but I take off my clothes anyway,
add them to the mound,
this little burial ground
called my past life.
A ten-day affair with reality.
Cleaning house at midnight,
I put things away,
a lover learning to live
alone again, but still dreaming
of the way only she could soothe me,
her body cold as glass.

The Broken Bowl

The broken bowl on the table
looks like two hands, gesturing,
trying to make itself understood.
I believe it wants to tell me
something about sorrow,
and sadness that cannot be overcome.
I lift the two halves
and hold them together
as if I were holding the dead body
of someone I loved.
I touch the broken edges gently
with a white glue that looks like sperm.
Now the bowl must learn again
to love itself, to acknowledge
the delicate place where it has broken
in half, to concentrate on what
cannot be forgotten or overcome.
For it is true:
This scar it will carry
into its second life.
The dark vein will always remain.
The bowl on the table has been broken
and will never be the same.

The Decoy

With his knife
he shapes the body,
turning the wood
gently in his hands.
Sanding it smooth,
he burns feathers
down the back,
paints the bird,
digs out a place
for the glass eyes.
Then he drops a pebble
into the hollow body.
My father could set it
adrift in the bay,
bringing birds down
for men to kill.
Instead, he places it
on the hearth
for his grandchild,
a decoy anyone can lift
and admire, something
he has made
that all agree is lovely,
could almost fly away.

The Hearing Aid

My mother – half-deaf,
a small metal box
pinned to her blouse,

and beneath the gray locks
the hidden earphone,
the wire running across

her heart to its home
in her ear – can barely
hear me anymore. I'm

just someone's voice
lost years ago, trying now
to make myself clear,

deliberately now,
so she will see how
hard the words come.

Bent to her breast, I speak
to the heart, almost hopeless,
where hardly anyone

is ever heard.

Portrait of My Father
and His Grandson

Because I love my father,
I can see him turning away
from the river and the divers
and the policemen and the red lights;
I can see him walking back
to the house, follow him
down the long hallway
to the child's room;
I can see him bending over
the empty bed and lifting
the heavy white spread
and carrying it back
to the river's edge
to wrap around his grandson.
But even though I love them both,
I cannot see why this should happen,
or tell you what the boy saw
under the water, or how my father felt
standing by the river when the divers came up,
or where he found the strength to survive
that night, hugging the wet body,
wrapping it up against the cold,
carrying it through the darkness,
home.

Apology to Andrew

Last night, I heard your mother,
my sister, crying in her sleep.
She was sleeping with my mother,
who is deaf, and did not wake
to comfort her. Mother and daughter
sleeping in one bed,
trying to make the world whole again.
My mother was there
to make losing you less
painful. But it is
painful. All day
they both had cried,
praying for strength.
I remember saying,
as though it would help,
as though it were true,
there is nothing we can do
to bring him back.
Now strength and rest will come
from what we suffer.
I even made a little metaphor,
stolen from the Bible:
the sun will rise from the darkness.
But last night, dreaming of you
lost in the river, your mother
kept crying,
your grandmother kept sleeping,

and I kept lying
there in the dark
as if I were you,
the dead child,
unable or unwilling to hear.
Andrew, I am sorry:
I always believed in words,
and sent them instead of my body
to comfort the ones I love,
your mother and grandmother,
my sister and mother,
and Andrew, I did not rise
to put my arms around them.

Leaving Town after the Funeral

After the people and the flowers
have gone, and before the stone
has been removed from your mother's house
and carved into a cross, I come back
on my way out of town
to visit your grave. And nothing
is there – only the ground,
roughed up a little, waiting for rain.
I sit down beside you
in my dark glasses
and put my hand on the earth
above your dead heart.
Two workmen are mowing grass
around the graves beside us.
They pretend not to see
I am crying. Quietly,
they walk over to their truck
to give me time.
The day is hot. They hold paper cups
under the water cooler on the flatbed
and drink together.
They are used to this.
The heat. The grief.
After a few minutes the younger one
walks back to work.
He gets down on his knees
and blows cut grass off a stone.
I believe he wants me to know

he will take care of you.
But hard as it is,
I know the truth:
when you drowned, your body
sank into the river forever.
Ten minutes to eight.
Darkness came down quickly.
And now it will be night
for a long, long time.
The workman gets up and goes on
with his work. I get up
and walk back to the car.
Andrew, we know the truth:
the cold child in the casket
is not the one I loved.

For My Sister

Because it was Christmas,
she planted a plastic tree
at the foot of the grave.
She asked her little boy
if he was being good,
then waited for him
to answer. After a moment
she smiled,
and laid the wrapped packages
on the cold ground.
These things she did
for herself. She knew
he couldn't hear –
he had the secret now,
attending to
the whispered words
and the gentle sobbing
that was becoming
a kind of music inside her.

Moving Day

Tomorrow our future begins, our lives
already defined by simple things
scattered on the lawn in sunlight.
Carrying small and useless
objects out to the car,
we dismantle our house
piece by piece,
brushing the dust of the past,
lifting each moment into the light.
You with the broken teapot,
I with the broken chair,
we bring all the old things with us
to begin our new life.
Back in the rooms we loved,
there's less and less of us to find.
We see only the space we wasted.
I look out the window and count
boxes waiting for the truck.
You see the room now
as it always could have been,
a vase of cornflowers and us.

Passion

A man casts the wide arc
of his passion, looking for something
to believe in again. And again
and again he is disappointed.
Eventually, his passion dies.
He begins to live
in the old way, as if she were still there –
work in the morning, afternoon in the garden –
but alone and without the old urgency.
Evenings he sits on the porch.
For the first time he has begun
to notice his neighbors –
the widow next door,
fathers coming home from the office,
the beautiful children.
He feels himself falling more and more
in love with these people,
no longer strangers to him,
and every evening,
he consciously breathes in the last
of the dying light, the passion
that will stay with him the rest of his life.

A Beginning

Today I am walking in woods
where men with chain saws
are felling trees and other men
with guns are killing deer.
Today I have nothing to praise
and nothing to feel sorry for.
Today I refuse to make the sky
tender or the earth heroic.
Today I will not condemn the trail
leading to the garbage dump
or lose myself in the leaves' fiery colors.
Today I won't pretend to understand
the ways we care for one another.
Today I will simply stand
in these thick woods and love
how the branches of one tree
reach into the branches of another.